Critics Rave

The book is great. I understand others a great deal better!
I. M. N. *Angstburger* (author of *Caring
Enough to be Conflicted*)

Don't wait to see the movie—read the book!
J. Mogul Ruthe

The advice in *Muppie* was very helpful, and I plan to use it for new policy
changes at MCCC.
John Lipp, Mennonite Cross-Culture
Committee

The chapter on the Muppie church deserves a great deal of critical thought
and attention.
Herb Dantzler, *The Mennonite Herald*

Muppie has profound theological insight. The footnotes are especially
helpful to the academic quest.
Willard Scott Smartly, ABCD Seminary

This book will encourage you in your spiritual journey.
Mary Ann Himm

The missiological insights related to the concept of redemption and lift are
staggering.
Saul Salunga

T·h·e

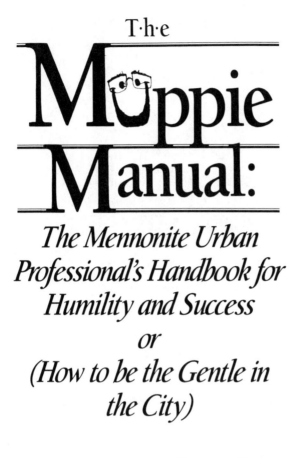

Muppie Manual:

*The Mennonite Urban
Professional's Handbook for
Humility and Success
or
(How to be the Gentle in
the City)*

Emerson L. Lesher, Ph.D.

Good Books

Intercourse, Pennsylvania 17543

(A word of thanks to our Yuppie attorneys who reviewed this manuscript for any libelous material. With all the Muppie attorneys running around these days, one can't be too careful.)

Design and illustrations by Craig N. Heisey.

THE MUPPIE MANUAL: THE MENNONITE URBAN
PROFESSIONAL'S HANDBOOK FOR HUMILITY AND SUCCESS
Copyright © 1985 by Good Books, Intercourse, PA 17534
International Standard Book Number: 0-934672-31-8
Library of Congress Catalog Card Number: 85-80988

Acknowledgments

I would like to thank the following people who have knowingly or unknowingly contributed to this project:

Luke Bomberger
Janna Books
Vince Books
Bill Boyd
Phyllis Boyd
Steven Denlinger
East of Plum Small Group
Elias George
Christine Goldberg
Nancy Heisey
Richard Heisey
Jeff Hyde
Sharon Hyde
H. Dale Kaufman
Stephanie Kaufman
Meribeth Sprunger Kraybill
Phyllis Kraybill
Ron Kraybill
Laura Lipkin

Larry Litwiller
Karen Reever
Brenda Regier
Michael Regier
Ken Ross
Pam Rutt
Roger Rutt
Donna Burkhart Shank
Roland Shank, Jr.
N. Gerald Shenk
Sara Wenger Shenk
Leon Stauffer
Jake D. Thiessen
Mary P. Thiessen
Janet Weber
John Weber
Phil Weber
William Whelihan

Thanks to the staff at Good Books: Craig Heisey, Donna Kunkel, E. Dean Mast, Mary Miller, Kenny Pellman, and Melanie Zuercher.

Special thanks to Merle Good and Phyllis Pellman Good who served as contributors, editors, and publishers for this project, and who also gave me much encouragement and confidence. They helped to make a period of crisis and transition more bearable.

Final thanks is to Ruth Detweiler Lesher who understood why this project was important, and who continues to give me the love and confidence to be more than I ever thought possible.

The following organizations did <u>not</u> sponsor or support this book in any manner:

—Institute for Mennonite Studies
—Mennonite Historical Society
—Mennonite Information Center
—Peace Section, Mennonite Central Committee
—Fellowship of Concerned Mennonites
—Student and Young Adult Services, Mennonite Board of Missions
—Choice Books
—Mennonite Mental Health Association
—Mennonite-Your-Way
—Reba Place Fellowship

Table of Contents

(Unfortunately, this book does not have the standard thirteen chapters which would make it easily usable as a Sunday school elective; however, this allows Muppie churches to schedule a silent retreat, a brunch, or a get-away weekend.)

Preface

The Mennonites are at it again! As if there aren't already enough Mennonite groups (the *Mennonite Yearbook* lists dozens of conferences and bodies), a new group known as Muppies (Mennonite Urban Professionals) has begun to emerge. But regrettably Muppies have received little attention from church leaders or institutions.

The goal of this book is two-fold:

(a) to help Muppies be the best Muppies they can be without being proud.

(b) to expose to the rest of the church (and, in particular, the parents of Muppies) what Muppies have been up to in the last 20 years.

I accept this task gratefully and with humility.

—Emerson L. Lesher, Ph.D.
Lancaster, Pennsylvania
June, 1985

A Word to Muppies

Since public confession is an important Mennonite quality, I would like to begin by listing several serious omissions of this book. I confess now, because as we all know, confession before an act is more acceptable than confession after an act.

1. I confess that I like the East Coast better than the West Coast (and this is even, or especially, after having lived in Los Angeles for five years).

2. I confess that I have been to Canada only four times in my whole life. (My apologies to Frankly Political Pepp.)

3. I confess that while some of my best friends are Mennonite Brethren and General Conference Mennonites, this book is about the Muppie phenomenon in the (Old) Mennonite Church. (For example, I keep hearing about the fast-track lifestyle of second- and third-generation Mennonite Brethren Muppies.)

I know that the eastern U.S. (Old) Mennonite establishment has often neglected the views of the fringe and marginal Mennonite groups to the north and west. However, as Mennonites we all know we must draw the line somewhere. Having drawn the line, however, I would be especially interested in hearing from Muppies outside the eastern (Old) Mennonite establishment since my next book is to be entitled *Minor Muppie Colonies Around North America.*

A Word To Parents

I think this book can be especially helpful to you. You have probably noticed that your children have gone through some changes in the past 20 years. For example, they may have changed from jeans to khakis, from long hair to styled hair, and from DCB (Draft Card Burner) to MBA (Master of Business Administration). Despite these changes, you may feel unable to relate to your Muppie children. This book should help you feel more comfortable with them, and help you to know what to cook and what subjects to talk about with them.

This book should also help you with those long silences and times of embarrassment which happen so often when meeting your child's Muppie or Yuppie friends. For example, one area of discomfort in the past has been knowing what to serve when eating together. For many years Muppies would not eat lettuce or Nestlé products because of boycotts and strikes; hence, there was much tension at the table. This book should make mealtime more enjoyable by explaining what Muppies like to eat and what they like to discuss. For example, broccoli is currently a favorite—Muppies will eat anything with broccoli in it.

However, I caution you as parents not to become too muppified. One reason (often the main reason) they come home is that they are homesick for the "Old Way" of doing things (many Muppies will not admit to this). Almost all Muppies get a kick out of showing their Yuppie friends what it is like "back on the farm." So one hint is to discontinue the gift subscription to *Guideposts* you gave your child, but to keep cooking those good old Pennsylvania Dutch meals.

A Word to Non-Mennonites

If by chance you are a non-Mennonite reading this book, we greet you.

What this book sets out to do is to show how Mennonites have become Yuppified. This may surprise you since most Mennonites are thought of as gentle people in rural areas. However, in recent years and in greater numbers, Mennonites are taking up the fast-track, aspiring, state-of-the-art ways of the Yuppies.

While for you, Yuppies are probably old news, you must realize that Mennonites have worked hard at not reflecting the current social values and patterns. Mennonites like to be several years, if not several decades, behind the majority culture.

While Mennonites are behind, they tend to eventually adopt the values and patterns of the larger society. But they also usually modify them to conform to more traditional Mennonite beliefs and patterns.

In general, books and articles on Yuppies do not intrinsically represent or describe the current Muppie phenomenon. Thus, I wrote this book to help identify some important distinctive characteristics of Muppies. For as an old Mennonite saying goes, "How can the world understand what it has not experienced?"

If you have trouble with some of the terminology in this book, please consult the Glossary. We regret that there is no 800 number or computer bulletin board to call to gain more information about Muppies.

How to Know If
You Are a Muppie

Below is a Muppie Scale to help you assess whether you are a Muppie. (If you think your child or sibling might be a Muppie, use this scale to determine their status.) Please answer the questions honestly—don't be humble in giving your responses.

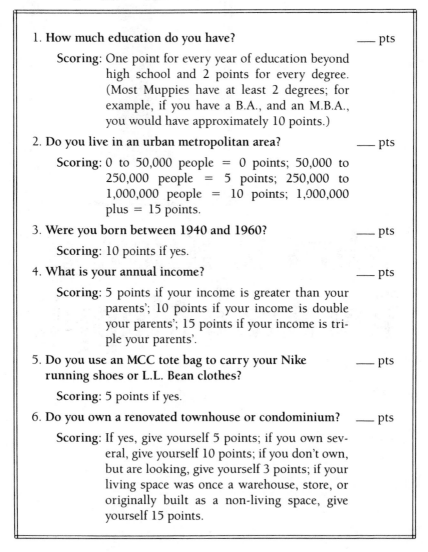

1. **How much education do you have?** ___ pts

    Scoring: One point for every year of education beyond high school and 2 points for every degree. (Most Muppies have at least 2 degrees; for example, if you have a B.A., and an M.B.A., you would have approximately 10 points.)

2. **Do you live in an urban metropolitan area?** ___ pts

    Scoring: 0 to 50,000 people = 0 points; 50,000 to 250,000 people = 5 points; 250,000 to 1,000,000 people = 10 points; 1,000,000 plus = 15 points.

3. **Were you born between 1940 and 1960?** ___ pts

    Scoring: 10 points if yes.

4. **What is your annual income?** ___ pts

    Scoring: 5 points if your income is greater than your parents'; 10 points if your income is double your parents'; 15 points if your income is triple your parents'.

5. **Do you use an MCC tote bag to carry your Nike running shoes or L.L. Bean clothes?** ___ pts

    Scoring: 5 points if yes.

6. **Do you own a renovated townhouse or condominium?** ___ pts

    Scoring: If yes, give yourself 5 points; if you own several, give yourself 10 points; if you don't own, but are looking, give yourself 3 points; if your living space was once a warehouse, store, or originally built as a non-living space, give yourself 15 points.

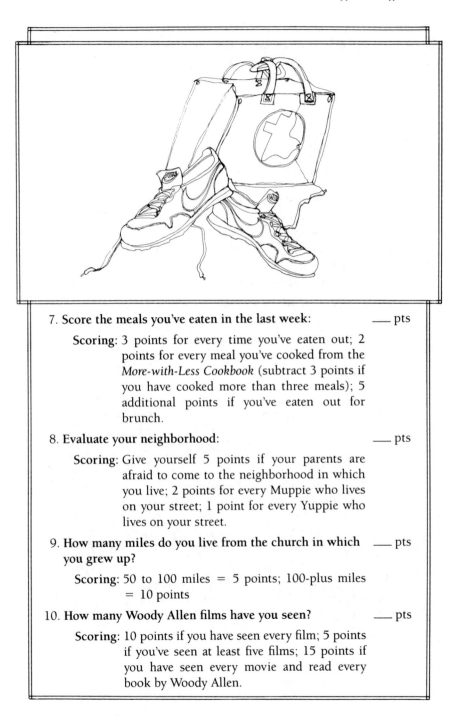

7. **Score the meals you've eaten in the last week:** ___ pts

   Scoring: 3 points for every time you've eaten out; 2 points for every meal you've cooked from the *More-with-Less Cookbook* (subtract 3 points if you have cooked more than three meals); 5 additional points if you've eaten out for brunch.

8. **Evaluate your neighborhood:** ___ pts

   Scoring: Give yourself 5 points if your parents are afraid to come to the neighborhood in which you live; 2 points for every Muppie who lives on your street; 1 point for every Yuppie who lives on your street.

9. **How many miles do you live from the church in which you grew up?** ___ pts

   Scoring: 50 to 100 miles = 5 points; 100-plus miles = 10 points

10. **How many Woody Allen films have you seen?** ___ pts

    Scoring: 10 points if you have seen every film; 5 points if you've seen at least five films; 15 points if you have seen every movie and read every book by Woody Allen.

11. **Did you belong to a social action group in college?** ___ pts

> **Scoring**: 5 points if you attended the May Day demonstration in Washington, D.C.; 5 points if you were arrested for a peace or social activity; 2 points for every demonstration you have attended.

12. **Do you wear blue jeans only on weekends?** ___ pts

> **Scoring**: If yes, score 5 points.

13. **Have you taken a European Anabaptist Tour?** ___ pts

> **Scoring**: If yes, score 5 points. If you also backpacked throughout Europe, add 5 additional points.

14. **Have you used your vacation days to protest national nuclear weapons policies?** ___ pts

> **Scoring**: If yes, score 5 points.

15. **Do you have at least three Jewish friends?** ___ pts

> **Scoring**: 2 points for each friend; 2 additional points if you have eaten blintz; 5 additional points if you like bagels and lox.

16. **Do you secretly listen to albums of Mennonite choruses?** ___ pts

> Scoring: 2 points for every album you've listened to in the last month (e.g., 500 Kansas Men Sing, The Choraleers, The Hartville Singers, Mennonite Hour groups).

17. **Have you seen a psychotherapist in the past two years?** ___ pts

> Scoring: If you've seen a psychologist, give yourself 10 points; if you've seen a social worker, 5 points; if you've seen a pastoral counselor, 2 points.

18. **Do you carry a business card?** ___ pts

> Scoring: 5 points if yes; add two additional points if it is engraved.

19. **Have you served with Mennonite Central Committee?** ___ pts

> Scoring: If you filed an application, give yourself 3 points; if you actually served, give yourself 5 points; if you served in an urban area, give yourself 10 points.

20. **If you are married, how much do you share household duties with your spouse?** ___ pts

> Scoring: Give yourself 10 points if you split chores 50/50; 5 points if you split chores 60/40; 0 points if you split chores 80/20.

To determine your Muppie Scale score, simply add the points from each of the 20 questions.

100–plus— Congratulations, you have come out from among them. You are a Muppie! This book will probably be very autobiographical.

70–99 — You are definitely on the track to becoming a humble and successful Mennonite Urban Professional. Go in peace.

40–69 — You are in the Muppie environment, but not of it.

0–39 — Be true to yourself and remember, the first shall be last, and the last shall be first.

If you feel guilty about the high score that you received on the Muppie Scale, we recommend the following procedures:

1. Discuss it with your small group and suggest that the group should hold each other more accountable.
2. Spend more time with your fast-track Yuppie friends so that you don't feel as guilty.
3. Go on a silent retreat.
4. Give another $50 to Mennonite Central Committee.
5. Learn how to rationalize better.

If you would like to improve your score we recommend the following procedures:

1. Attend a Muppie congregation.
2. Get another degree.
3. Read *Fortune* magazine and *Sojourners* simultaneously.
4. Read books on Anabaptist history.
5. Start networking with Yuppie friends.
6. Begin calling noodles "pasta."
7. Move to a larger city.

Defining the
Problem

The Muppie phenomenon (as defined on the facing page) has received little attention by most observers, but may yet shake the Mennonite community to the core. Few books or articles have addressed the issue[1]; there have been no Laurelville conferences, pamphlets, or study papers on this topic. Why have church leaders been silent? What is this phenomenon and how can we better understand it?

Even publications which see themselves as "progressive" (e.g., *Festival Quarterly*[2]) have not focused on this issue. Is the church asleep or only denying its present situation? Who will address this deviation squarely and without compromise? Have we slipped away? Have we become both Catholic and Protestant in our views of correct doctrine and proper Christian decorum?

The definition of a Muppie is like all good Mennonite things—*plain* and *simple*; however, in reality, being a Muppie is more than meeting the demographic criteria listed in the definition. It is both a lifestyle[3] and a worldview[4]. In this study, a wholistic[5] approach will be taken to describing the Muppie; hence, the demographic characteristics, as well as the lifestyle and the worldview of the Muppie, will be outlined.

As you read you will discover what all too many have discovered, that

Definition:

Muppie or Muppy (mup-ē) n., pl.—
ies. 1. Persons born between 1940 and
1960, who are children of Mennonite
parents, were raised on a farm or in a
rural environment, and are now professionals living in an urban environment.
2. Former Yuppies who have become
Mennonites [etymology is unknown;
however, oral histories have traced its
usage to several Mennonite professional
communities. See Yuppie (Young Urban Professional), Yap (Young Aspiring
Professional), Preppie].
Synonyms: Mumpie (Mennonite Up-
wardly Mobile Professional), Mapie
(Mennonite Aspiring Professional),
Mebbie (Mennonite Baby Boomer).

—From *The New Mennonite Dictionary
and Almanac*

while Muppies appear to be successful and aspiring young professionals, they are deeply "conflicted."[6] Symbolic of this conflict is that Muppies often hold *Sojourners* in one hand and *Money* magazine in the other. While the Bible says not to let your right hand know what your left hand is doing, too frequently the brain remembers. Muppies know the first shall be last and the last shall be first, but they have also learned that it is best to make hay while the sun shines.

Notes

1. An exception is an article entitled "Urbanization of Mennonites: Canadian and American Comparisons," *Mennonite Quarterly Review*, 1982, 56, 269–290. This is required catechism for all Muppie applicants.
2. The editor indicated that the topic is too hot to handle in most circles, and that several Mennonite church leaders had been approached, but they all refused, saying, "The time is not right. It is too divisive an issue. We must move toward consensus before this topic can be discussed." This is another example of how even Muppie publications have been cautious to speak the truth in love.
3. A. Radical Gish, the eternal non-Muppie and un-non-Muppie, first coined the term "lifestyle."
4. The term "worldview" is a technical term that has been introduced into the Mennonite vocabulary by anthropologists such as D. Carlos Jacobs in his book, *A Separate Worldview*.
5. "Wholistic" is also a commonly used Muppie word. It should not be confused with "holiness" as emphasized by John Wesley.
6. "Conflicted" is a frequently used Muppie word and has spiritual, psychological and social implications. This subject is discussed in a recently discovered and soon-to-be-published manuscript entitled, *The Recovery of the Conflicted Anabaptist Vision* (by you-know-who).

Seven Muppie
Variations

Up to this point we have been discussing the generic Muppie; however, there are really several different variations of Muppies. The reasons for the many Muppie variations are multiple, complex, and interrelated; for example, one could point to Muppies' geographic regionalism, their reaction against parental advice or what their advisor in college recommended, pride, life course experiences, and providence (or luck, as some Muppies are inclined to believe).

1. The Professional Muppie

In many respects, this is the "real" Muppie. This Muppie includes your run-of-the-mill doctor, lawyer, accountant, junior executive, manager, psychologist, social worker, and dentist. While these persons tend to work in the "service" professions, they tend to make more money than any of the other Muppies. Money management and tax deductions are a common concern and point of discussion for these Muppies. **These Muppies tend to:**

a. Have a quilt and/or antiques in their office.
b. Talk about how great it is to walk to work.
c. Run at the Y at lunchtime.
d. Work 50 to 60 hours a week.
e. Read *The Other Side* magazine and feel guilty.
f. Give money to Mennonite Central Committee.
g. Take "Get-Away Weekends."
h. Talk about planting a garden but never do.
i. Unashamedly read *Wall Street Journal*.
j. Get a lot of invitations for credit cards.
k. Start Clifford Trust funds for their children.
l. Call their account executive or broker regularly.
m. Be on financial and physical plant committees of their congregations.
n. Think the church should have more seminars on ethical decision-making.

2. The Academic Muppie

This Muppie is a professor, researcher, teacher, or graduate student. This Muppie thinks he or she should make as much money as the Professional Muppie, but would never admit it. The Academic Muppie is always taking a course or two, and parents (and friends) have a hard time understanding why it is taking this Muppie so long to get out of school. **These Muppies tend to:**

a. Read the *Mennonite Quarterly Review*.

b. Have taken an Anabaptist Tour.
c. Take painting jobs in the summer.
d. Have the complete works of Menno Simons.
e. Have studied in Boston.
f. Have attended Associated Mennonite Biblical Seminaries for at least a year.
g. Read *New York Review of Books*.
h. Find "eating out" an existential and intellectual experience.
i. Work at writing an article or book on "Anabaptism/Mennonites and Anything."
j. Have floor-to-ceiling bookshelves in their living rooms.
k. Have personal computers.
l. Prefer spending money on books rather than on food.
m. Have all of the books written by John Howard Yoder.
n. Use words ending with "a," like "data," "vita," "phenomena," "bacteria," and "criteria."

3. The Radical Muppie

This Muppie is a professional radical who works for a political or social organization that is attempting to change or address a large national or international problem or conflict. This Muppie usually makes very little money, but feels guilty about every cent earned. **Some characteristics of Radical Muppies are that they:**

a. Are knowledgeable about all social issues, boycotts, strikes, and human rights violations.
b. Are well versed in statistics.
c. Know the holdings of multinational corporations better than most stockbrokers.
d. Travel a lot.
e. Attend a lot of conferences and demonstrations.
f. Were arrested at least once.
g. Have lived in Washington, D.C.
h. Read *Sojourners*.
i. Are expert letter writers to government officials (if they don't have their Senators' addresses memorized, they have them taped to their refrigerators).
j. Have the largest garden possible in the city.
k. Ride a bicycle or take public transportation.
l. Make other Muppies feel uncomfortable.
m. Read books written by retired military officers.
n. Use words ending in "nt", like "disarmament," "movement," "judgment," "covenant," and "commitment."

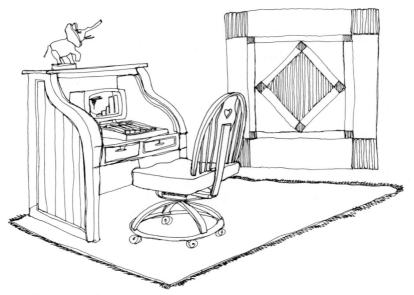

4. The Church Muppie

This Muppie works for a church or para-church organization or agency. This Muppie has usually completed a graduate degree in theology or social science and is now an Associate Director of Generic Ministries. This Muppie is willing to work at a reduced salary for a few years because he/she knows that he or she can make more money in future years as an Academic or Professional Muppie.

Closely related to the Church Muppie is the Muppie Pastor. Although similar to the Church Muppie, the Muppie Pastor usually has a Master of Divinity degree from a Protestant divinity school. In the past the Church and Pastor Muppies have been primarily men; however, in recent years, more women are becoming such Muppies. **Some characteristics of Church Muppies are that they:**

a. Read both *Christian Century* and *Christianity Today*.
b. Belong to a family that includes a lot of church leaders.
c. Are thinking of getting a Ph.D.
d. Use words ending with "ing", like "facilitating," "resolving," "resourcing," "processing," "tithing," "sharing," and "discerning."
e. Unlike other Muppies, have been known to buy clothing at MCC Self-Help Shops.
f. Served for several years in another country.
g. Are likely to buy a double house with another Muppie couple.
h. Like to combine church conferences with extended family vacations.
i. Have a lot of international art objects.

5. The Artistic Muppie

This Muppie is a painter, writer, singer, actor, craftsperson, or other artisan whose primary income is derived from artistic activities. Artistic Muppies tend not to work with traditional Mennonite art forms such as quilting or woodworking, but instead have chosen more typical and classical art forms and media.

It is difficult to comment on the income of Artistic Muppies since it varies a great deal, usually depending on the degree to which they have popularized their art. However, in general, this Muppie makes less than other Muppies, except for the Radical Muppie. **Artistic Muppies tend to:**

a. Have lived in New York City or at least make a lot of trips there.
b. Have given a presentation at The People's Place.
c. Have created a logo for a church agency.
d. Make banners for their congregations.
e. Attend a lot of art museums and galleries.
f. Have a studio or office in a townhouse or a warehouse.
g. Have a lot of paintings and wall hangings of various kinds in their living space.
h. Feel that the church does not appreciate the value and ministry of art.
i. Incorporate a lot of agricultural themes in their artistic work.
j. Keep odd hours.
k. Often be art brokers for Professional Muppies.

6. The Non-Muppie Muppie

These people are often confused with real Muppies. Actually they live in the city because they enjoy it and for no other reason. In this sense they are more honest than real Muppies.

(Most Muppies enjoy the city, but usually don't admit they are in the city primarily to have fun. Most Muppies try to justify their being in the city with a fancy religious, psychological, or occupational scheme, like "It is where I can best be used," or because they think Mennonites have been too isolated in the past.)

Non-Muppie Muppies tend to have less education and to be less aspiring than real Muppies; hence they make less money (but that's okay with them). **Characteristics of the Non-Muppie Muppies are that they:**

a. Are more "laid back" and not as goal-directed as other Muppies.
b. See a lot of films.
c. Go to art exhibits with Artistic Muppies.
d. Take long walks in the park.
e. Go to a lot of free or city-sponsored events like concerts, restaurant

fairs, health fairs, and garden tours.
f. Don't carry a calendar or business card.
g. Are Type B personalities.
h. Read *People* and *Rolling Stone* magazines.

7. The Non-Urban Muppie

In the last several years, there are a growing number of people who fit this category. These are people who are muppified and very urbane in their tastes and lifestyle, but who live in a rural area or small town (however, they never live in suburbia). TVs and expressways have had a great deal to do with the rising number of Non-Urban Muppies. Non-Urban Muppies have these characteristics. **They:**

a. Lived in an urban area for several years.
b. Are part of a family business that does not permit them to live in the city.
c. Take a lot of pleasure and get-away weekends to the city.
d. Have a lot of business contacts in large cities.
e. Read the same books and magazines as real Muppies.
f. Relate primarily to other Non-Urban Muppies.
g. Would rather (and often do) travel an hour to eat at a French restaurant instead of driving 15 minutes to eat at the best "Mennonite Family Restaurant."
h. Daydream about living in the city.
i. Are often consulted by non-Muppies regarding how and where to do things in the city (i.e., How do you get to the zoo?).

Are the Muppies Anabaptists? Were the Anabaptists Muppies?

Since Mennonites can only take so much humor and wit until they catch themselves and begin to ask serious spiritual questions, this chapter will deal with the tough issues. Here are questions to think about (and even discuss with your small group):

1. Do Muppies follow in the tradition of Conrad, Menno, Pilgram, H.S., Guy, J.C., and J.H.Y.?
2. Are Muppies faithful to the Anabaptist Vision?
3. Is there a place within our story of faith for Muppies, or must they go a separate way?

Downtown Zurich (1520s A.D.) The Muppie World of Conrad Grebel

Key
1. Small group met here every other Thursday night.
2. Often had brunch here with Felix.
3. Favorite bookstore and newsstand.
4. Farmers' market where he got his broccoli.
5. Site of debates with Yuppie Ulrich.
6. Running paths of Conrad.
7. Favorite croissant shop.
8. Watery location where friend Felix was conflicted.

4. Would Conrad feel more comfortable under the forebay or on an elevator?
5. To which world are Muppies conformed?
6. Are Muppies living off the interest of their heritage? Are Muppies rich in all ways because of the sacrifices and nonconformity of their parents and grandparents?
7. Can the Anabaptist Vision only be recovered in Elkhart or Harrisonburg?

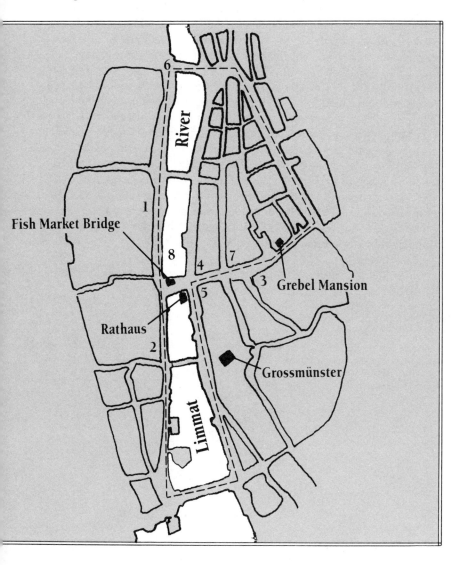

Who will answer these questions? Just as the bishops used to be the gatekeepers of the faith, today the scholars (theologians, historians, sociologists, and psychologists) have been called in from the bullpen to decide where to draw the lines. Ultimately, it will be the academicians who must decide if the Muppies are faithful to the Anabaptist tradition. But while we wait for the scholars to process these questions about Muppies, there are several points which beg for our attention:

1. First, historical analysis indicates that many early Anabaptist leaders were well educated urbanites. For example, Conrad Grebel grew up in an upper class Zurich family and attended universities in Vienna and Paris; Hans Denk was educated at the University of Ingolstadt and lived in Basel; Pilgram Marpeck was a civil engineer in the city of Strassburg and probably attended the Rattenberg Latin School; Obbe Philips was a surgeon and barber; and Dirk Philips was a Franciscan who probably had formal theological training. In addition to these early leaders, historians believe that there is evidence to suggest that a significant number of later Anabaptists were Muppies. For example, the Anabaptist movement started primarily in larger European cities (Zurich, Bern, Strassburg, Amsterdam, etc.), and in a study of social origins of Swiss Anabaptists, 20% were found to be urbanites, with a significant percentage being intellectuals and clergy[1].

2. Most Mennonite scholars are Muppies, or at least are closely associated with Muppies (after all, a lot of scholars started Muppies on their way). Therefore, can we really trust the scholars to critically evaluate whether Muppies are part of the Anabaptist story? (Would you let your banker audit the bank books?)

3. Do Muppies really want to be part of the recovery of the Anabaptist Vision? Or has it become an Anabaptist nightmare for some?

Note

1. For more details, see C.J. Dyck's *An Introduction to Mennonite History*, C. Krahn's article "Dutch Mennonites Prospered in Golden Age," *Mennonite Weekly Review*, 1980, 58, 6. and P. Peachey's two works, *Die soziale Herkunft der Schweizerischen Taufer in der Reformationszeit*, Karlsruhe, 1954; "Social Background and Social Philosophy of the Swiss Anabaptist," 1925–1940, *Mennonite Quarterly Review*, 1954, 28, 102–127. If you are still not convinced, read *The Apocrypha*.

A Short Account
of Muppies in
Modern History

In the last 80 to 90 years Mennonites have begun a movement toward urban areas (in addition, urban centers in some parts of North America have moved out to meet the Mennonites). In general this has created a greater Muppification of the Mennonite Church.

There have been several waves or generations of Mennonites who have moved to the city. While this book focuses on the second wave, there was one primary earlier wave.

Muppies of the First Wave were born before 1940 and tended to become Muppies because of a "call" they first felt during 1-W or Voluntary Service. While some First Wave Muppies continue to be involved in service, many have become quite successful and professional people.

Today, First Wave Muppies often play the role of "expert" in the church. Every church committee, institutional board, seminar, and conference needs an "expert" member; thus, First Wave Muppies often find themselves in these positions.

Another role played by First Wave Muppies is that of connector between the traditional Mennonite community and the "world." As connectors they communicate Mennonite values and practices to the world, and communicate back to the church (especially to its leaders) the values and changes of the larger world.

How to Identify First Wave Muppies:
1. They are over age 45 and, with rare exceptions, married males.
2. They have at least 18 years of education.
3. They served in another country for at least three years.
4. They are frequent speakers at church conferences and seminars.
5. They are on numerous church institutional boards.
6. They have siblings who are farmers.
7. Their children attend an Ivy League college.
8. They drive a large, new, usually American car.
9. Their spouse is currently completing a B.A. or M.A. degree, usually in art, theology, or counseling.
10. They tend to live in a more suburban area, or in single detached houses (not in townhouses or in a marginal or gentrified neighborhood).
11. They tend to disagree with siblings about whether their parents should stay in their own home or go to a retirement community. First Wave Muppies either think their parents are fine and that their close siblings should simply see their parents more often, or believe that their parents are unable to care for themselves and are being neglected by their siblings and so should be placed in a retirement community.

The Muppies described in this book are actually the Second Wave of Muppies in modern Mennonite history. Some important differences between the First and Second Waves are that the Second Wave had the First

Wave as models, and that the reasons for becoming muppified are different for the Second Wave. For example, many Second Wave Muppies had siblings or other family members who became physicians, or who, after 1-W service, started an occupational therapy supply business that now has branches in most Midwestern and Northeastern cities.

Mennonites tend to become Muppies today not because of a "service" impulse, but for one or several of the following reasons: (a) to find oneself; (b) to prove that Mennonites are not backward; (c) to express oneself; (d) because farming is too expensive; (e) because one is too lazy to milk cows 14 times a week for 52 weeks a year; (f) to keep from being part of an isolated community; (g) to help change oppressive social systems.

While it is beyond the scope of this book to discuss all things Muppie in the Mennonite Church, I do want to mention that there is a Third Wave of Muppies currently in formation. These persons are under age 25 and are the children either of First Wave Muppies, or of parents who lived in rural areas, but not necessarily on farms. Their socialization process has been quite different from that of other Muppie Waves. For example, Third Wave Muppies are too young to know what or who the following are: Vietnam, Watergate, Richard Nixon, the Chicago 8, the Beatles, Rebirth, Bob Dylan, sit-ins, Gloria Steinem, draft cards, the *Post-American,* bell-bottoms, the Black Panthers, and real blue jeans. The Third Wave Muppies tend to be more punk and chic whereas the Second Wave are more radical and hip.

The Separate in the City: Muppies vs. Yuppies

A definitive study of the differences between Muppies and Yuppies (Young Urban Professionals) has yet to be conducted (anybody looking for a dissertation?).[1] In general, the external differences between a Muppie and Yuppie are subtle and only a matter of degree. For example, Yuppies wear Brooks Brothers clothing, whereas Muppies wear Jos. S. Banks clothing; wealthy Yuppies drive BMWs, whereas wealthy Muppies drive Saabs and Audis; Yuppies vacation in Bermuda, whereas Muppies visit their siblings in Haiti who are missionaries. Yuppies buy townhouses in gentrified neighborhoods, whereas Muppies buy rowhouses in marginal neighborhoods (sometimes fixing them up to sell to Yuppies); and on Sunday, Yuppies read the Sunday newspaper and go to brunch, whereas Muppies go to church, then go to brunch and finally read the Sunday newspaper.

Listed below are some additional external differences between Yuppies' and Muppies' possessions and practices:

Yuppies	Muppies
Racquetball on Sunday	Basketball on Saturday
Health club	YWCA or YMCA
Pro bono	Mennonite Disaster Service
Financial consultant	Small group
Psychonanalysis	Family therapy
Vacation condominium	Cooperative log cabin
Independent	Democrat
$30,000-plus a year	$20,000-plus a year
American Express Gold Card	American Express Green Card
Original painting	A lithograph
Jacuzzi	Claw-foot bathtub
Neiman-Marcus catalog	Land's End catalog
IBM PC	Apple
Hardwood floors	Pine-wood floors
Architectural Digest	_Metropolitan Home_

The internal processes and experiences of Muppies and Yuppies are different in some important ways. Yuppies and Muppies were both influenced in the 1960s and early 1970s by the popular thought about materialism and the simple life. But a primary difference between the two groups is that while Muppies come from a long religious and social tradition which has stressed modesty and thrifty living, Yuppies did not grow up in this atmosphere. Yuppies can be concerned with ethical decisions and how they use their money, but Muppies are generally more conflicted on these issues. Consequently, Muppies often go through a spiritual, psychological, and social process of "justifying" their decisions. For example, Muppies may spend and use their money in a similar fashion to Yuppies, but they usually feel more guilty about it.

Muppies and Yuppies also behave differently when they are angry or in a competitive situation; Yuppies are outright aggressive, whereas Muppies are passive aggressive.

A final difference between Yuppies and Muppies, which has both internal and external implications, is that Yuppies grew up in the suburbs, whereas Muppies have never lived in suburbia. In fact, one point that draws Muppies together is their common disdain for almost everything suburban—shopping malls, expressways, split-level houses, American station wagons, and cultural homogeneity. It is interesting to note that while Yuppies grew up in suburbia, few affirm that lifestyle, and many are attracted to the rural-urban transition of the Muppies.

More than one Yuppie has been envious of the Muppie who lives and works in the city, but who spends holidays and weekends visiting the family farm, for who wants to return to the family patio or shopping mall fountain? Suburbia is foreign to the experience of most Muppies, and most of them want to keep it that way.

Questions for discussion:

1. Can a Yuppie become a Muppie?
2. Can a Muppie become a Yuppie?
3. Should the Student and Young Adult Services discourage people from becoming Yuppies? If so, how?
4. Should the commission on church growth attempt to evangelize Yuppies by using Muppies?

Note

1. If you are seriously thinking about a dissertation on this topic, you should read "Ideology, Family and Group Identity in a Mennonite Community in Southern Ontario" by D. Appavoo in the *Mennonite Quarterly Review*, 1985, 59, 67–93. Or you might consider doing a follow-up of the subjects in the P.M. Lederach study, entitled *Mennonite Youth* (Scottdale: Herald Press, 1971). Lederach observed Mennonite youth in the late 1960s, many of whom have now become Muppies. Completion of such a study would no doubt make you a big hit in the academic and church institutional circles. You might even get a job offer.

The Formal Training of the Muppie

Education is central to the Muppie experience. In fact, it is difficult to believe that one can be a Muppie without having at least one college degree. This is not because Muppies are so much smarter or brighter than non-Muppies, but because education is primarily a socialization process. Education is the "home" of Muppie-ism. It is here that rural Mennonite students first learn about and assimilate the worldview and lifestyle of the urban professional.

The socialization process takes many forms but usually includes IDS lectures, Study-Service Trimesters, urban semesters, First Wave Muppies, professors who travel a lot and have large libraries, cultural series, films, and classes on Anabaptism (see Exhibit One on page 47).

An additional part of the socialization process for many Muppies is attending a non-Mennonite institution, usually for graduate school (see Exhibits Two and Three and their accompanying explanations on pages 48–52). This experience frequently brings Muppies in contact with Preppies and Yuppies, which serves to introduce Muppies to middle class and even upper class values. The Preppies and Yuppies usually further educate these Mennonites to such things as the virtues of wine and cheese, the best places to shop, good tax shelters, and where and how to tip.

While most Muppies attended Mennonite colleges for their undergraduate training, an increasing number of persons are attending non-Mennonite colleges. There are many reasons for this, not the least of which are the following:

1. Their parent teaches at a Mennonite college.
2. It's more expensive to attend a Mennonite school.
3. A non-Mennonite college is closer to the family business.
4. They don't agree with the theological position of most Mennonite colleges.
5. Mennonite colleges don't have the major that they wish to take (architectural engineering, for example).
6. They want to go to law school at Harvard and think that a degree from Northwestern would look better on the application than a degree from Goshen College.

However, the most important reason that Mennonites attend non-Mennonite colleges and universities is that they are actually fast-track Muppies who can't wait to be further muppified. Hence, they speed up the process by not going to a Mennonite college in order to be more quickly socialized into the arts, ethnic foods, health spas, townhouses, foreign films, crime, pollution, and cultural diversity found in urban areas.

While Mennonite colleges have attempted to "expose" students to urban life and its issues, a better strategy[1] would be to move Goshen College to Chicago, Hesston College to Wichita, and Eastern Mennonite College to Washington, D.C., and to have students go to Goshen, Hesston, and Harrisonburg for rural work-study semesters. This would no doubt curb the declining enrollment in Mennonite colleges and generally aid in the muppification of the Mennonite Church.

How to Address an Educated Muppie

This section is especially for the relatives and former Sunday school teachers of Muppies, who wonder how to address them (in person or on paper), and how to introduce them to others. There are several general principles to follow regarding titles:

1. Most Muppies prefer not to be called Brother or Sister.
2. Equality of titles and first names is very important among Muppie couples.[2]

3. In general, no title or "Ms." is preferred over "Miss" or "Mrs." among Muppie women.
4. Muppies like others (except patients or clients) to call them by their first name.
5. Muppies like people to know that they have advanced degrees, but want that fact made known in a way that is unassuming.
6. For parents who would like to introduce their children's achievements, it is preferable to say, "My daughter has a doctorate," rather than, "My daughter, Dr. Margaret Rohrer."

A Special Case

Let's say Muppies Rachel and Jonas Hess both have doctorates. How should you address one or both of them?

Totally Unacceptable:

Dr. and Mrs. Jonas Hess
Mrs. and Dr. Jonas Hess
Dr. and Dr. Jonas Hess
Mrs. Jonas Hess
Mr. Rachel Hess

Somewhat Unacceptable:

Dr. and Dr. Rachel and Jonas Hess

Preferable:

Rachel and Jonas Hess
Rachel Hess
Jonas Hess

Notes

1. "Strategy" is another commonly used word among Muppies. "Strategy" is discussed in a helpful manner in a recently published book, entitled *Strategizing in Your Dreams: Climbing Jacob's Ladder* by A.B.C. Schmidt.
2. This point should be especially useful for church colleges and institutions. You would think such organizations would be sensitive to the use of titles and names; however, Muppies have not found this to be the case. The maiden names of many married women have been totally destroyed. For example, if Betty Beiler, who graduated from Eastern Menno Simons University (EMSU), married Henry Hess and mailed a contribution to EMSU, the receipt would probably say, "Thank you, Mrs. Henry Hess" (not even "Thank you, Mrs. Betty Hess" or, more appropriately, "Thank you, Betty Beiler Hess"). This is one of the few things that Muppies get really angry about.

Exhibit One: Fact Sheet
Eastern Menno Simons University

Enrollment:

Men–450
Women–700

Racial Breakdown:

White–1118
Black (Africa)–25
Black (U.S.A.)–5
Asian–2

Religious Denominations:

Mennonite Church–800
General Conference Mennonite Church–39
Baptist Church–99
United Methodist Church–118
Non-Denominational Churches–94

Majors:

Pre-med	Nursing
Psychology	Sociology
Pre-law	Pre-MCC
Mennonite history	Radical economics
Agroeconomics	Womenite studies
Family business management	Education
Mathematics	Chemistry
Computer science	

Campus Attractions:

Rural atmosphere
Small town
Mennonite home cooking
Mennonite dating partners
Basketball champions: Simons Simpletons
Singing group: EMSU Recruiting Chorale
Alumni magazine: *Humility Echoes*
Yearbook: *The Annualbaptist*

Scholarships:

J. Abner Yoder Scholarship: For students from Ohio who plan to return
to Ohio to construct windmills.

Sister Emma Detweiler Scholarship: For women in the top 10% of their class who demonstrate promise in computer science and homemaking.

Jakob Hochstetler Heritage Scholarship: All students who are descendants of Jakob Hochstetler may apply.

Exhibit One: Explanatory Data

Mennonite colleges have been important institutions in advancing the Muppie lifestyle and worldview. In recent years there have been numerous changes in college life and curriculum. First, there has been a trend toward more women and fewer Mennonites. There has also been the addition of some new majors which are more consistent with Mennonite understanding of a liberal arts education (i.e., Radical Economics, Pre-MCC, and Womenite Studies).

Exhibit Two: Vita

(The circled numbers refer to the explanatory paragraphs on the facing page.)

Name: Mary Muppie Miller
Place of Birth: Intercourse, PA
Date of Birth: November 16, 1952
Address: 777 South St., Baltimore, MD ⑨

Education

Dates	Institution	Major	Degree
1957–1966	Locust Grove Mennonite School	—	—
① 1967–1970	Lancaster Mennonite High School	Academic	H.S.
1970–1972	Eastern Mennonite College	English & Bible	—
② 1973–1975	Goshen College	④ History	B.A.
1975–1976	Mennonite Biblical Seminary	Peace Studies	—
⑥ 1978–1980	University of Illinois	Psychology	M.A.
1980–1982	Temple University	Psychology	⑧ Ph.D.

Masters Thesis: Cohesion and Conflict Among Mennonite Families

Dissertation: Social-Cultural Determinants of Depression Among Mennonite Young Adults

Honors and Scholarships

Junior Herdsman Award, 4-H
⑤John Horsch Peace Essay Contest, Goshen College

Mennonite Mental Health Scholarship
Who's Who in Mennonite Schools
Ford Foundation Scholarship

Employment

Part-time Positions

Family Farm—Laborer
Willow Mountain Farms—Baker's assistant
Spruced-Up Camp—Camp counselor
Kauffman's Fruit Farm—Apple picker
Neiman-Marcus—Waitress
Pillhaven Hospital—Recreation Assistant
Brookstone—Clerk
Merrill Lynch—Clerical Assistant

Full-time Positions

1981–1982: Bellevue Park Hospital, NY, NY—Psychology Intern
1982–Present: Baltimore Mental Health Center, Baltimore, MD
⑩ 1983–Present: Private Practice, Inner Harbor Medical Plaza, Baltimore, MD

Publications

Why Mennonites Don't Like Themselves. _Gospel Herald_
Depressive Features of a Sect in Transition. _Journal of Abnormal Psychology_

Other Experiences

③ 1972–1973: European Trainee Program, Mennonite Central Committee
⑦ 1976–1978: Program Director, Philippines, Mennonite Central Committee
⑪ 1984–Present: Coordinating Team, Front Street Community Mennonite Church

Exhibit Two: Explanatory Data

1. While Mary wanted to attend a Mennonite elementary school, she did not want to attend a Mennonite high school. However, her parents and bishop convinced her it was really the only option for a young Mennonite girl.

2. Mary considered attending a state college, but instead chose a Mennonite college for several years since her friends were going to a Mennonite college. She liked reading novels and was concerned about peace issues so she majored in English and Bible.

3. Mary tired of school, so she dropped out to travel in Europe and see all the things she had been reading about (art and Anabaptist history). Since

she didn't want to go on her own, and since she could travel at little personal expense, she went under Mennonite Central Committee.

4. Mary decided to return to college, but her interests had begun to change. She had become more concerned about political and social issues and believed that if she was really serious about being a Christian, sensitive to the current state of affairs, she should major in history. She also decided she wanted a broader approach and so went to a Mennonite college in Indiana.

5. After winning a friendly little competition on peace, Mary graduated with a B.A.

6. The more she studied, however, the more she realized that, rather than history, it is theology and ethics that hold life together and make it meaningful, so she went to seminary.

7. After being in seminary for only a year, Mary discovered that theory is not enough, that talk is, in fact, cheap. Theory and praxis must go hand in hand, she reasoned, so she went to the Philippines with Mennonite Central Committee for two years.

8. While in the Philippines she started to see that it is nearly impossible to change large social systems. She saw more hope in attempting to change individuals, so when she returned to the U.S., she completed a doctorate in psychology.

9. Mary moved to Baltimore after a year of internship in New York City, because it was close, but not too close to her home community. In addition, Baltimore is becoming, now increasingly, a Yuppified city.

10. Mary now has a private practice in addition to her regular job (amounting to a total of about 55 hours of professional work a week) so that she can pay off nine years of school debts, meet her mortgage on her recently purchased townhouse, and buy a Toyota Camry.

11. Mary is on the coordinating committee of Front Street Mennonite Church where she is one Muppie among many, and leads a group on "How small groups can help you overcome your depression."

Exhibit Three: Resumé

(The circled numbers refer to the explanatory paragraphs on the facing page.)

Name: Bob Bmup* Brubaker
Date of Birth: January 17, 1948
① Place of Birth: Pigeon, MI
Social Security: 666-0000-66
⑤ Married: Brenda Troyer Brubaker
Children: Sara, Joshua

Goals: To find a management position with a growth industry company that is state-of-the-art in production and marketing. Prefers company that has positive community relations and is environmentally concerned. Willing to relocate.

Skills: Financial Analysis, Systems Analysis, Production Planning, Management

Education:

Date	Institution	Major	Degree
③ 1968–1970	Hesston College	Business	A.A.
1970–1975	State University of Michigan	Business	B.A.
1977–1979	Northwestern University	Management	M.B.A.

Employment:

② 1966–1968:	Evening Manager, Brubaker's Poultry, Pigeon, Michigan	
④ 1970–1977:	Assistant Manager, Brubaker's Poultry, Pigeon, Michigan	
1979–1981:	Production and Systems Planner, Purina Chow, Chicago, Illinois	
⑥ 1981–1984:	Senior Production Supervisor, Purina Chow, Chicago, Illinois	
1985–Present:	Chief, Production Planning, Purina Chow, Chicago, Illinois	

Organization and Associations

Mennonite Economic and Development Associates
Rotary International
⑦ Board Member, Southside Community Improvement Council
Board Member, Mennonite Central Committee, Midwest Region
Member, Coordinating Team, Chicago Mennonite Community Fellowship Church

Hobbies

Sailing, gourmet cooking, running, collecting old weather vanes

References are available on request.

*Business Mennonite Urban Professional

Exhibit Three: Explanatory Data

1. Bob grew up in a small rural Mennonite community and attended a local public school. However, the flavor of the school was decidedly Mennonite since over half the students and several of his teachers were Mennonites.
2. After high school Bob stayed home to work in the family poultry busi-

ness. His parents, however, wanted him to take a two-year business course in college so he could return and help manage the business. Bob did not know if he wanted to stay in business. He did know he did not enjoy school. But since he didn't know what else he wanted to do, he went to college.

3. During the first two years of college he warmed up to both school and business and decided to complete college.

4. But by this time his parents wanted him to return to the business, since it was growing rapidly (besides, two years of college was two more than Bob's dad had had). Although he didn't want to, Bob returned home to help manage the business, but also took evening classes and finished his college degree.

5. After graduating, Bob married Brenda Troyer who had just received her Masters in social work two years before. While Bob tried to make life exciting, he had a harder and harder time. He tried to stay with the family business but his sights were higher. He was restless, so he and Brenda started to take extended weekend trips to Chicago where they really enjoyed themselves.

6. Bob finally left his home community the way so many do, by going to school. Bob returned to school for his MBA and has been slowly progressing up the corporate ladder at Purina Chow in the chicken feed production and marketing area.

7. Bob has been trying to integrate the Mennonite world and values he learned in Pigeon with the professional business world by serving on several boards of Mennonite organizations. Even Bob's hobbies represent the values and activities of his two different worlds.

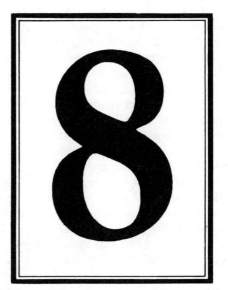

The Muppie
Church

The Mennonite Church is a primary institution in the life of Muppies. This is true for those who do not attend a Mennonite Church any longer, and for those who continue to be involved. Those Muppies who are no longer involved usually continue to discuss the implications (usually negative) of having been brought up in a close, isolated, restrictive, and non-enhancing environment. Those who are actively a part of a congregation often talk about *why* they are still involved. Despite this, Muppie congregations have continued to grow, until today most major cities in the U.S. have a Mennonite congregation or fellowship.

Some persons have explored the possibility of forming a Muppie Conference, while others think it should only be an association or informal group (e.g., an Association of Muppie Congregations and Fellowships). Some have even gone so far as to suggest that membership in the Muppie Conference or Association should be dependent upon a congregation or fellowship scoring an average of at least 70 on the Muppie Scale.

There are at least three levels of church involvement among Muppies:

1. **The Ethnic Muppie**—These Muppies consider themselves Mennonites, but not necessarily Christians, and usually do not "identify" with any particular congregation. Usually Ethnic Muppies visit their home congregations once or twice a year and go to the annual Mennonite Central Committee Relief Sale. Ethnic Muppies have a large circle of Muppie friends whom they consider the "church."

2. **Muppie Member**—These Muppies attend and are active in congregations made up of other Muppies. Such congregations usually have one of two histories: (a) a former city mission started by a single woman in 1926 that has now been totally taken over by Muppies, or (b) a planted community church that was started for and by Muppies in the past ten years. Such congregations were first started by a student and young adult services group, but then became congregations with memberships in both the Mennonite Church and the General Conference Mennonite Church. Muppie members in these congregations talk about such things as the lack of models of faith in the city, how best to organize themselves for the work of the church, what they really believe, how great it is not to have the "baggage" of traditional congregations, and how to support one another.

3. **Muppie-as-Minority**—These Muppies attend older non-Muppie Mennonite congregations. These Muppies are usually openly frustrated with church and see themselves as a "witness."

Parallel Characteristics Between Muppie and Non-Muppie Congregations:

Non-Muppie	Muppie
Personal devotions	Spiritual disciplines
Sunday school	Educational experiences

Benches	Folding chairs
Sunday afternoon dinner	Small groups
Evangelism	Outward journey
Pastor	Coordinator/moderator
Song leader	Worship leader
Revival meetings	Retreat
Communion	Celebration
Tithing	Economic sharing
Special offering	Jubilee Fund
Bible study	Biblical interpretation
Personal witnessing	Theological discussion
Council meeting	Accountability
All-day meeting	Resourcing seminar
Sewing circle	Craft night
Mimeograph machine	Copier
Prayer	Inward journey
Tent meeting	Block party
Sermon	Input
Commitment	Ethical responsibility
Fellowship	Community
Mennonite Central Committee	Mennonite Central Committee
Missionary	Missiologist/Anthropologist
Piano or organ	Guitar
Prison ministry	Victim Offender Services
Pulpit	Kitchen stool
International lesson	Lectionary

What Muppie Congregations Have That Non-Muppie Congregations Don't Have:

Liturgical movement
A computer
An expert on everything
Long-range planning committee
Banners
Celebrations such as Martin Luther King Day

What Non-Muppie Congregations Have That Muppie Congregations Don't Have:

Head coverings (as in some faithful Lancaster Conference churches)
Regular attendance
Old people
Sunday school opening
Funerals
Vacation Bible School

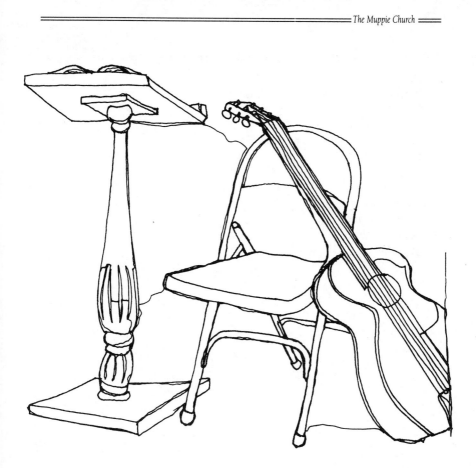

Favorite Muppie Theological Themes or Issues

1. Peace and justice
2. Believers' church
3. Priesthood of believers
4. Incarnation
5. Hermeneutics
6. Spiritual formation
7. Sexuality
8. Money and power
9. Discernment of gifts
10. Biblical feminism
11. Grace
12. Psychological growth
13. Artistic expression and faith

57

Biblical or Theological Issues or Themes Not Discussed by Muppies

1. Demonology
2. Prophecy (or the Second Coming)
3. Spiritual warfare
4. Speaking in tongues
5. Submission (chain of command)
6. Predestination
7. Miracles
8. Heaven
9. Modesty
10. Ten Commandments
11. Soul-winning
12. Types in the Old Testament
13. Revival

Muppie Cuisine
and Garb

Consumerism, and in particular the purchasing of appropriate cuisine and attire, are important to the Muppie lifestyle. There are certain principles by which Muppies buy and consume:

1. Never buy anything gaudy or gauche.
2. Buy a few quality items rather than many inexpensive items.
3. Always consult *Consumer Reports.*
4. If you can share it with your small group, then you can buy the deluxe model.
5. If it symbolizes traditional Mennonite simple life values, you can pay more for it (i.e., a quilt, dry sink, or a black Saab with black bumpers).
6. Buy only natural items.
7. Spend more if it can help you live more simply (e.g., a coffee-maker with a timer).
8. Buy it if it improves the quality of your intrapersonal and interpersonal life.
9. Buy it if you wouldn't be embarrassed if your Muppie friends learned that you had it.

Muppie Cuisine

Eating is serious business for Muppies. The percentage of their income that Muppies spend on food is similar to the percentage of work time that their grandparents put into growing, preserving, and preparing food.

Muppies are concerned that food be fresh, natural, and low in calories (except for desserts, which are supposed to be fattening). The more expensive the ingredients, and the more exotic-sounding the name, the greater the possibility that Muppies will eat it. It is just as important for Muppies to have croissants for breakfast as it was for their grandparents to have had shoo-fly pie. Two cuisine traditions which have greatly influenced Muppies are gourmet cooking and the use of natural foods.

Favorite and Frequent Muppie Foods

Croissants	*More-with-Less* casseroles
Häagen Dazs ice cream	Fish
Cheese (imported)	Gourmet take-out food
Poultry	Paté
Chocolate chip cookies	Stir-fried anything
Junk food*	Artichokes
Pasta	Bagels
Fresh vegetables	Rice
Guacamole	

*Muppies won't eat it in public or admit to eating it.

Favorite Beverages

Diet Coke with lemon	Fruit juice (especially freshly squeezed)

Skim milk
Espresso
Sparkling cider
Decaffeinated water-
    processed coffee blends

Bottled water
Herb tea
V-8 Juice
Beer (lite or imported)
Chablis

What Muppies Don't Eat

Jello
Red meat
Chow chow
Pot pie
Canned vegetables

Noodles
Mashed potatoes
Stewed pretzels
American cheese

What Muppies Don't Drink

Kool-Aid
Punch

Chocolate milk
Hard liquor

Books Found in the Muppie Kitchen

Baking with Earthware
Using Cuisine Art
More-with-Less Cookbook
The 60-Second Gourmet
Back issues of *Bon Appétit*

The Enchanted Broccoli Forest
Whole Foods for the Whole Family
The New York Times Cookbook
The Mennonite Community Cookbook

Dining Out

Unlike their parents and grandparents, Muppies usually eat out at least three or four times a week. Muppies dine at all types of eateries with the exception of Mennonite family restaurants, hotel cafés, and suburban chain restaurants. Below are appropriate Muppie eateries matched to the proper occasions:

Breakfast
Family-owned coffee shop downtown
Bakery/deli, or any place selling croissants

Lunch
Jewish/Italian deli
Outdoor café
Croissant shop

Fancy Dinner
French restaurant
Continental restaurant
Any restaurant which takes only American Express

Quick Dinner
Gourmet cafeteria
Fancy sandwich shop

Brunch
Any lunch or dinner place listed above is acceptable; however, an outdoor café is preferable.

Eating with Friends
Chinese restaurant
Mexican restaurant
A pub

Things Muppies Don't Do in an Eatery
Clean their plates
Pray (moment of silence, maybe?)
Wrap up the bread and take it home
Make small talk with the waiter/waitress
Leave a tract

Muppie Garb

Each Muppie variety wears clothing appropriate to their identity and lifestyle. (For example, the Radical Muppie and Church Muppie do not wear pin-striped suits to work, whereas it is acceptable for a Professional Muppie to dress that way.) An exception, however, is corduroy jackets and even corduroy suits, which are acceptable for just about any type of Muppie. Tweed jackets and skirts are also commonly acceptable Muppie garb. In general, Muppies tend to be more Preppie than Yuppie in how they dress. For example, most Muppies maintain the standards of dress as outlined in *The Official Preppy Handbook,* edited by Lisa Birnbach (© 1980 by Lisa Birnbach, Workman Publishing, New York. Reprinted with permission of the publisher.). They include:

1. Conservatism
2. Neatness

3. Attention to detail
4. Practicality
5. Quality
6. Natural fibers
7. Anglophilia
8. Specific Color Blindness
9. The Sporting Look
10. Androgyny

Especially important for the Muppie are conservatism, practicality, quality, and natural fibers. Contrary to what most parents or grandparents might think, Muppies dress rather conservatively. Their clothes are modest, and not faddish. For example, tweed jackets and three-button suits can be worn for several decades and still be stylish and acceptable.

Muppie clothes are practical because they are designed with the four seasons in mind, and layering, which is a common Muppie practice, allows for varying indoor and outdoor temperatures. For example, if you visit a Radical Muppie who keeps the thermostat at 60 degrees, you retain all layers of clothing; however, if on your way home you visit a Professional Muppie who keeps the thermostat at 68 degrees, you simply remove several layers of clothing.

Quality is important since everything needs to be well made. Muppie clothes are bought to last and retain their simple and understated style.

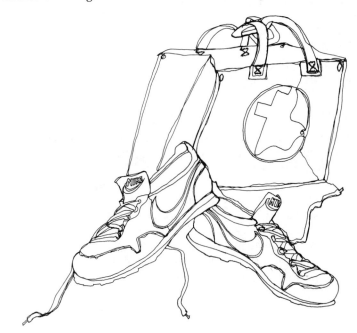

Natural fibers such as wool, cotton, silk, and lambswool are preferable. Of course, belts and shoes should be constructed of only real leather. Double-knit, polyester, and nylon fibers are totally unacceptable.

While Muppies deny it, and most non-Muppie Mennonites aren't aware of it, the principles by which both these groups buy and wear clothing are very similar. For example, the dress of most conservative Mennonite and Amish groups could be described as conservative, practical, and of high quality, and many include natural fibers. In this sense, many Muppies follow in the tradition of having a distinctive and uniform garb.

What Muppies Wear to Work

Wool trousers or skirt	Pin-striped suit
Silk tie	Tweed coat
Button-down Oxford shirt	Silk shirt dress
Blue blazer	Grey flannel suit
Khaki suit	

What Muppies Wear for Casual Attire

Hand-knit wool sweater	Cotton jogging suit
Corduroy jacket	Khaki trousers or skirt
Blue blazer	Cotton turtleneck
Tucked shirt	Shirt dress
Straight-leg Levi jeans	Jean skirt

What Muppies Wear to Church

Same as Casual Attire

Muppie Shoes

Classic pumps (navy, black, beige)
Oxfords
Nike running shoes
Any L.L. Bean shoe
Docksiders
Weejun loafers
Most any Pappagallo shoe
Foulweather boots

Muppie Accessories

Straw basket bag
Leather briefcase
Pearls
Earrings (simple gold or silver)
Rings (only wedding rings)
Knit wool scarf
Bow ties (women or men)
Long ties

Mennonite Central Committee or L.L. Bean tote bag
Coach bag

Accessories Worn Only Occasionally or Not Used at All
Cuff links
Circle pin
Hair bands
Tie clips or tacks
Collar pins
Elegant lighter
Key chain
Plastic shopping bag
White leather belt or shoes for men

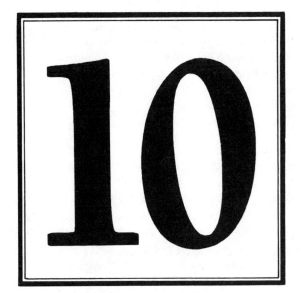

The Muppie
Living Space &
Lifestyle

While renting one's home is acceptable, it is not preferable, and most Muppies are at least looking to buy living space. A not uncommon Sunday afternoon activity is attending Open Houses. Muppies may find their living space in townhouses, condominiums, converted warehouses, carriage houses, and various types of historic landmarks.

Listed below are some characteristics of Muppie living space. This is a guide for how to renovate living space, or what to look for in buying a Muppie living space.

There are several acceptable interior design motifs that Muppie living space can follow but, in general, the primary design themes are primitive, country, and high tech.

Regardless of the theme, furnishings or features are bought with two things in mind: (a) utility, and (b) aesthetic or artistic value. While the grandparents of Muppies bought furnishings simply for their utility, Muppies now buy them for their aesthetic and artistic value as well. Things are not only bought to be used, but to be appreciated and enjoyed.

What to Look for in Muppie Living Space

Natural wood floors	Exposed brick
Skylights	Fireplace (for atmosphere, not heat)
Quilts	Track lighting
Folk art	Rugs (braided, rag, oriental)
Family antiques	MCC Self-Help craft items
High ceilings	Ceramic tile
White or off-white walls	Landscaped garden
Outside deck	Industrial kitchen equipment
Butcher block counter tops	Original or unique features*

*These are especially good for conversation starters

Things Not Found in Muppie Living Space

White venetian blinds	Drop ceiling
Paneled walls	Wall-to-ceiling mirrors
Shag carpeting	Crystal chandeliers
Aluminum siding	Fake brick
Religious wallhangings	Calendars
Plastic furniture	Linoleum

Advanced Technology in the Muppie Living Space

VCR	Phone-answering machine
Computer	Coffee grinder
Pasta machine	Stereo system
Beeper from office	TV with remote control

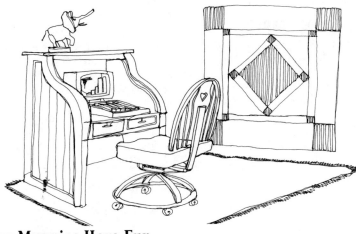

How Muppies Have Fun

Muppie Music

As in most other areas of life, Muppies appreciate only the best, and music is no exception. While they have a wide range of interests and favorites, they listen only to the classics in the field. Since Muppies have little listening time they must select the best there is. The types of music that Muppies choose most often are classical music, rock and roll, bluegrass, folk music, and jazz.

What Muppies Don't Listen To

Punk rock music
Disco
Easy listening or elevator music
Broadway musicals
Popular Christian music
Christian rock

Muppies' Favorite Singers or Groups*

Cat Stevens
Crosby, Stills, Nash & Young
Rebirth
Bob Dylan
Three Dog Night
Credence Clearwater Revival
Peter, Paul & Mary
John Prine
Pete Seeger
The Beatles

*Most Muppies believe the best music was written in the 1960s and early '70s.

The Muppie Schedule

Just as the parents and grandparents of Muppies used to work long hours on the farm, Muppies tend to work long hours and are very busy people. However, while their parents and grandparents used to keep time by the seasons or by church holidays and family occasions, Muppies keep time with calendars and datebooks.

In fact one can tell a great deal about Muppies by the units of time displayed in their datebooks. For example, do they have a month-at-a-glance, a week-at-a-glance, or a day-at-a-glance, and is each day divided

	Sunday	Monday	Tuesday
Social Calendar for a Childless Muppie Couple		1 Exercise Class	2 Meal with Horowitzs
	7 1:30 Film matinee	8 Worship Group meeting	9 Computer class
	14 Silent retreat	15 Exercise class	16 7:30 Merrill Lynch - Account Executive
	21 Family Get-Together	22 Exercise Class	23 Computer class
	28 11:30 Brunch with Yoders	29 VACATION	30 VACATION

into 60-minute units, 30-minute units, or 15-minute units?

It is not uncommon to have to schedule work and social events several weeks in advance with most Muppies. Muppies usually never agree to anything without first saying, "I'll have to check that date." Some Muppie small groups have been known to take several hours to try and coordinate their schedule and plan for the next meeting.

Part of Muppie etiquette is to impress others by developing subtle and unassuming methods of letting others know how busy they are.

Wednesday	Thursday	Friday	Saturday
3 Class on prayer	4 Meal with Small Group	5 Shopping	6 6:00 Dinner & play with Millers
10 Class on prayer	11 Marital therapy - Dr. Fritz	12 Party at work	13 Silent Retreat
17 Class on prayer	18 Small Group	19 Pick up video of The Big Chill	20
24 Class on prayer	25 Freeze Walk Meeting	26	27 Paint church center

How Muppies Relax

Even when relaxing, Muppies are usually goal-directed and prefer quality. Hence, they attempt to use their time wisely. Their relaxation often includes:

Exercising
Refinishing furniture
Remodeling their townhouse
Working in their landscaped garden
Taking classes
Programming their computer
Reading the latest best-selling business book

Muppie Vacations

Vacations are usually connected to some other activity:

—a professional or business conference
—visiting family in another country
—working on a project or writing a book
—visiting Muppie friends in another city

Because of the nature and demands of their work, Muppies usually take long weekends instead of extended trips. They also like to stay in bed and breakfast inns or old classic hotels.

What Muppies Do for Entertainment

View films (Muppies never refer to films as "movies," and they especially enjoy art or foreign films)

See plays (usually they have season subscriptions)

Attend art exhibits

Gather with other Muppies and sing from *The Mennonite Hymnal*

Eat out with Muppie and Yuppie friends

Listen to "A Prairie Home Companion"

Magazines Muppies Subscribe to

Sojourners
*Wittenburg Door
Ms. Magazine
Mother Jones
Anything with "New" in the title:
  *Sunday *New York Times*
  New York Review of Books
  The New Republic
  New Oxford Review
  New Shelter
  New Body
The Other Side
Festival Quarterly

Country Living or *Metropolitan Home*
Mennonite Central Committee Peace Section Newsletter
Mennonite Central Committee Women's Newsletter
Gospel Herald
*Consumer Reports
**Glossy regional magazines, (e.g., Philadelphia Magazine, Washingtonian)*
Harvard Business Review
Popular Computing

*What Muppies actually read

What Muppies Don't Read

Reader's Digest
Mennonite Weekly Review
U.S. News and World Report
Hot Rod
Good Housekeeping

National Enquirer
With
Popular Mechanics
National Geographic
Guideposts
Moody Monthly

Books on the Muppie Shelf

A History of Art and Music by H.W. Janson and Joseph Kerman

An Introduction to Mennonite History by C.J. Dyck

The Politics of Jesus by John Howard Yoder

Happy as the Grass Was Green by Merle Good

New Left and Christian Radicalism by Art Gish

Future Shock by Alvin Toeffler

The Secular City by Harvey Cox

The Greening of America by Charles Reich

The Grapes of Wrath by John Steinbeck
Beyond the Rat Race by Art Gish
Rich Christians in an Age of Hunger by Ronald J. Sider
The Yuppie Handbook by M. Piesman and M. Hartley
The Christian Way by John Miller
Animal Farm and *1984* by George Orwell
Zen and the Art of Motorcycle Maintenance by Robert M. Pirsig
Herbs and Plants among the Plain People by Clair Mellinger
Our Bodies, Our Selves by the Boston Women's Health Book Collective
All We're Meant to Be by Nancy Hardesty and Letha Scanzoni
The Cost of Discipleship by Dietrich Bonhoeffer
Sex for Christians by Lewis Smedes
The Foxfire Book by Elliot Wigginton
The Meaning of the City by Jacques Ellul
The Recovery of the Anabaptist Vision by Guy F. Hershberger
The Concept of Dread by Soren Kierkegaard
Perils of Professionalism by Donald Kraybill and Phyllis Pellman Good
A Portrait of the Artist as a Young Man by James Joyce

What Muppies Drive

While the parents and grandparents of Muppies are known for their large, American, four-door, black or dark blue cars, Muppies are becoming known for their high quality, high performance, sporty, sedan foreign cars. It is difficult to find a Muppie who drives an American car. If one does, it is probably because of a recent dissolution of a household community which had an old American-made station wagon. However, in most cases Muppies trade up.

Muppies' cars usually include air conditioning and an AM/FM stereo; however, unlike their Yuppie friends, Muppies consider a car phone, leather seats, and personalized plates extravagant features. Some Muppies, however, do feel justified in getting a sun roof if they do not get air conditioning. Muppies tend to order grey, blue, black, or plum-colored cars, and many prefer the black bumpers, customarily a part of those vehicles.

Popular Muppie Cars

Low income Muppie cars
Used Japanese cars
Used European cars
Middle income Muppie cars
New Japanese cars
Favorites are Honda Accord, Toyota Corolla or Subaru station
wagon
New European cars
Favorites are VW Rabbit or Jetta

High income Muppie Cars

    Most any new European car
    Saab
    Volvo
    Peugot
    Audi

Influential Theologians Among Muppies

Muppies like to drop the names of certain theologians; however, just because Muppies drop these names doesn't necessarily mean that they have actually read their books. Because Muppies are so busy they usually have a big stack of books by these theologians that they intend to read:

John H. Yoder	Martin Marty
Jacques Ellul	Virginia R. Mollenkott
Jim Wallis	Henri J.M. Nouwen
Ronald Sider	Karl Barth
Walter Brueggemann	Willard Swartley
Daniel Berrigan	Marlin Miller
Dietrich Bonhoeffer	Elizabeth O'Connor
Reinhold Niebuhr	Richard Foster
Thomas Merton	Howard Snyder

Organizations Muppies Belong To or Give Money To:
Amnesty International
Smithsonian Institution
Their local YMCA and YWCA
The American Civil Liberties Union
Save the Whales
Voice of Calvary
Public Radio and TV stations
Mennonite Central Committee

Organizations Muppies Don't Belong To or Give Money To:
Moral Majority
National Rifle Association
Daughters of the American Revolution
Campus Crusade for Christ

Businesses Muppies Are Not Involved In:
Pet food
Avon
Amway
Anything made of plastic (except computers)
Fast foods
Military/defense industry
Mary Kay Cosmetics

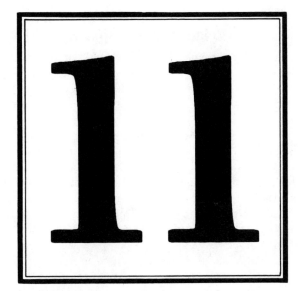

Muppie
Relationships

"Relationships" are what Muppies do with other people: their friends, children, parents, and especially their spouses (or potential spouses). Muppies, as in other areas of life, have high hopes and goals for their relationships and desire quality, and relationships that are meaningful and enhancing.

A Muppie's Relationship: A Spouse or "Significant Other"?

Unlike their Yuppie friends who have "significant others," Muppies have "spouses" (Muppies don't use the words "honey" or "dear," and only "wife" and "husband" occasionally). While living together has been known to happen to more than one Muppie, the norm is for most Muppie couples to marry.

Before marriage, Muppie couples do not "date"; instead, they "have a relationship." This relationship may go on for an extended period of time and between several cities. Muppies tend not to be out looking for a relationship, but are ready if someone comes along. They tend to continue on with their life's goals, and if they meet a partner along the way, so much the better. Muppies are not usually overly anxious about their relationships and when asked about them they will say, "Time will tell," or "We'll have to wait and see."

While it is not as difficult as it used to be, Muppies still find it hard to find other Muppies to marry. Muppies marrying Muppies is usually the preferred arrangement. However, to find another person who is (a) Mennonite, (b) urban, (c) professional, and (d) lives in the same city, or is willing to move to the same city, is often a difficult task. Muppies who marry Muppies tend to have met at college, at a Muppie church, in Voluntary Service, or in an intentional community.

The decision to get married is done after great deliberation (and, frequently, psychotherapy) and strategizing as to who would be the most appropriate spouse, and who would best help them to accomplish their life goals. The reasons Muppies are attracted to each other and eventually marry may be a bit different than for non-Muppies.

While romance and physical attraction can never be underestimated in a Muppie relationship there are other important qualities or characteristics that Muppies look for in selecting a spouse. For example:

1. Compatibility
2. Quiet possessiveness but not jealousy
3. Friendship—love and marriage are seen as an extension of friendship
4. A reciprocal relationship
5. The ability to share deep emotions
6. Strong intellectual capacity
7. A similar approach to life—goal-directed and an achiever
8. A similar mission in life

Some qualities which are not important, or are less important to Muppies in selecting a spouse, are:

1. Love at first sight
2. Great sex[1]
3. High level of continued romantic excitement
4. Perfect physical form
5. Possessiveness or dependency
6. "Game" playing—such as flattery, coyness, etc.

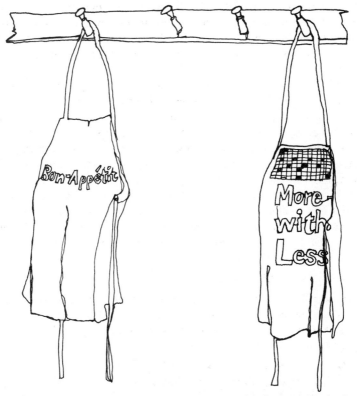

There are four types of Muppie marriages. The first type, which is also the most common, is the Dual Career Marriage. This is where both spouses have well-identified and clearly distinguished professional careers, or at least one spouse is actively working in his or her professional area while the other spouse is in graduate school.

A second type of Muppie marriage is when one spouse is a Professional, Academic, Artistic or some other type of Muppie, while the other spouse is a Displaced Muppie. A Displaced Muppie has left the marketplace to be the primary caregiver for the couple's children. The Displaced Muppie works part-time or has taken a sabbatical and plans to return to full-time Muppie service.

A less common type of Muppie relationship is the Commuter Marriage. Here spouses can pursue their professional goals and careers. They get together often on weekends or for three- or four-day weekends.

The fourth type of Muppie marriage is the Mixed Marriage. In this case, Muppies marry Yuppies or Preppies, usually because the Muppie partner was unable to find another Muppie partner. Hence, he or she developed a relationship with a Yuppie or Preppie.

Mixed marriages among Muppies appear to be a growing phenomenon. While (Old) Mennonites have not empirically observed this issue, one of the more "fringe" groups, in Manitoba, discovered that inter-marriage between Mennonites and non-Mennonites was found to increase with urbanization[2].

Another distinction of Muppie marriages is that often the woman hyphenates her maiden name with her married name, or only uses her maiden name. It is quite Muppie for the man to also use a hypenated combination of his own last name and his wife's maiden name. This practice has become quite common, especially for persons who have two short last names. However, it is less frequently done by persons who have long, many-syllabled last names.

This practice can often cause much embarrassment. Family and friends find it difficult to know how to introduce such individuals or couples. And even Muppies find it awkward to introduce these people. Many Muppies, however, find this practice an important social, theological and sexual statement about who they are.

Signs of a Liberated Muppie Couple

A major influence on Muppie thinking and, in particular, on Muppie relationships has been feminism. Most Muppies at least report that they believe in the equality of the sexes. Here are some ways to know if they practice what they preach:

1. Do spouses share driving when riding together?
2. Do both have similar years of education?
3. Do both have well-defined careers?
4. Do both spouses have an apron hanging in the kitchen (and are both equally dirty)?
5. Do Muppie mothers "parent" and Muppie fathers "babysit"?
6. Do both share packing their children's lunches?
7. Do both spouses have life insurance policies?
8. Do both have an IRA?
9. Do each have the same number of credit cards?
10. Do they share household tasks evenly[3]?

What has been covered so far is not to imply that there are no single Muppies, for there are many. To be a single Muppie is quite acceptable; in fact, Muppies seldom pressure single Muppies to marry. A common goal among single Muppies is to develop meaningful and deep relationships with other Muppies. It has been noted that while Muppie couples eat out often, this occurs with even greater frequency among single Muppies who are socializing.

Marital problems and divorce are not foreign to Muppies. Many Muppies even believe that it is abnormal not to have been to a marital therapist. Although Muppies like to read books on marital problems and communication, they tend not to attend Marriage Encounter or Marriage Enrichment. When a Muppie couple is having problems or is getting a divorce their Muppie friends usually: (a) recommend that they see their therapist (if they are not already); (b) urge that they talk to their small group; (c) suggest a book on how to communicate better (usually this is introduced by, "This is not your typical Christian book, but it may be helpful"); (d) do not take sides with either partner (want to remain neutral); and (e) are not "condoning" or "judgmental." Muppies who divorce often use a mediation service or have an out-of-court settlement rather than an ugly court battle. Property is usually divided evenly and, if there are children, joint custody is usually awarded.

Muppie Children

After marriage a second major developmental crisis for most Muppies is whether and/or when to have children. This decision is usually processed for several years between spouses as well as with their small group and Muppie friends.[4] However, the decision to have children is usually not consummated until the woman has worked several years within her profession.

If the decision has been made to have children, then many additional decisions are processed so as to give the potential child the best and most enriching childhood and education experience possible. One of the first decisions has to do with the child's name. Listed below are some common Muppie names.

Sara	Jonathan
Rachel	Nathaniel
Joshua	Hannah
Aaron	Josiah
Benjamin	Rebecca

Any Old Testament name is acceptable and is preferable over other types of names, including New Testament names. Names which are totally unacceptable for Muppie children include the following:

Harold	Tony	Emerson	Ricky
William	Wilma	Gidget	Ralph

An apparent common concern for many Muppie parents is that their children should have the advantages and enriching experiences that they never had as farm or rural Mennonites. Because of this, Muppie children often appear to have much power in influencing decisions as to how the family spends its time and money. Few children are denied experiences which will enhance their self-concept, intellectual abilities, social awareness, and cultural appreciation.

Activities to enhance and enrich the Muppie child's life include the following:

Suzuki violin or piano lessons
Infant swimming lessons
Ballet lessons
Educational toys
Personal computer and software
Educational camps
Day-care center with a French name
Personal tutor

Muppie parents do a lot of reading about developmental stages and theories. If their child does not reach a particular stage in time they become quite concerned. Muppies are also likely to seek professional help if this goes on for too long. If a Muppie's child is "ahead" of the stage, Muppies have subtle and humble ways of informing their friends.

While Muppie parents try to have "quality" time with their child, they are also quite anxious about whether they are adequate parents. Muppies like to continue to second-guess themselves about their own parent practices, attitudes, and styles. While Mennonite parents used to have siblings and grandparents to consult about parenting, Muppies now have small groups and professionals for this function.

Muppies who are parents, and particularly those who are Displaced Muppies, are usually:

1. Writing a book.
2. Spending their time "meaningfully."
3. Taking up artistic pursuits they didn't have time for before.
4. Concerned for the first time in their life about Sunday school.
5. Deciding that pets are the best dynamic equivalent to growing up on the farm.
6. Using a 30-number programmable phone, 20 numbers of which are programmed for babysitters and day-care centers.

At this point in time it is difficult to tell what will become of the children of most Muppies. However, there are at least three possibilities:

1. The children of Muppies will remain Muppies. If this happens we would expect some of these children to win a Nobel or Pulitzer Prize in future decades.
2. Move back to the country and drop out of professional life.
3. Worst of all, move to the suburbs.

Muppie Relationships with Family and Friends

While the families of Muppies may not believe it, Muppies are quite interested and fascinated by their family roots. While Muppies may have chided their parents or aunts and uncles for always asking or inquiring about the kinship ties of various people, Muppies now do a similar activity. However, they refer to it as family systems analysis or oral history. For Muppies, the goal is often to become differentiated from their family roots, rather than staying connected to them.

The Many Social Worlds of the Muppie

While the parents of Muppies may have one or two (maybe three at the most) primary circles of people to which to relate, Muppies often have many worlds of family and friends. Listed below are some of those worlds that any one Muppie might have, and some of their common activities:

World	Activities
Home church (church where Muppies grew up)	As little as possible
Extended family (Mennonite and Amish)	Reunions (1 at Christmas and 1 in the summer)
Family of origin	Phone or visits on weekends
Family of procreation	Home management and parenting
Muppie friends	Small group, films, eating
Co-workers	Work, party
Neighbors	Shovel snow, organize around an issue
Yuppie and Preppie friends	Eat, play Trivial Pursuit
Muppie Church	Retreats, coordinating meetings

Relating to these worlds consumes enormous amounts of time and energy, and can make one schizophrenic. It may be difficult for the Muppie to share with one world what it is like in the other worlds. (There are times when others don't even know how to ask the right questions). And sometimes Muppies don't want to, or are afraid to share with one world that they are also part of another world. In each sphere the rules and worldview are quite different.

Living in different worlds can make anyone do funny things, such as hiding things. However, hiding things from particular guests has a long history in Mennonite families. Just as Mennonites used to hide the radio and TV from the bishop, Muppies hide things from their families and friends (be they Muppies or Yuppies). Listed below are some such things:

    * Wine
*, ** Tapes on real estate deals with no down payment
    ** *The Bible* and Sunday School Study Guide
    ** *U.S. News & World Report*
    * VCR tapes of *Everything You Wanted to Know About Sex*
*, ** Old Mennonite Quartet albums
    * Pipe

Key
 *Family
**Friends

Additional Muppie Tensions and Burdens

As you can see, there is a dark side to being a Muppie. One serious need most Muppies feel is to find at least one other Muppie one can trust, with whom to discuss the difficulties of living at the interface of many worlds.

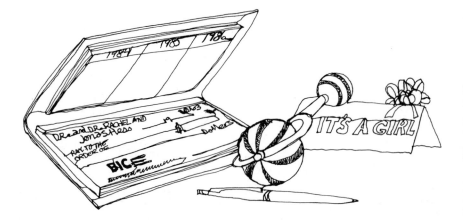

Certain issues burn deep into Muppies' brains and surface occasionally when Muppies of like mind meet:

What to do with the family farm?

Should we raise our children in the city?

Should we send our children to a public or Mennonite school?

How to tell my parents my brother is gay?

How to look like you are living both simply and elegantly at the same time?

What values of the past should be retained?

How to pass on a distinctive heritage?

Should we invest in high yield mutual funds or in socially conscious mutual funds?

Notes

1. It is difficult to comment on the sexual habits of Muppies, either before or after marriage. There is little or no hard data on this aspect of Muppie life, and in consulting several professional and lay persons on the sexual activity of Muppies there was no consensus as to what kind, how much, when, or where Muppies engage in sexual activity. Several persons did suggest that Muppies are often too busy to have sex. This may account for the low birth rate among Muppies. Clearly much more research is needed on this sensitive topic.

2. L. Driedger, R. Vogt & M. Reimer, "Mennonite Intermarriage: National, Regional, and Intergenerational Trends," *Mennonite Quarterly Review*, 1983, 57, 132–144. The ethnic and religious contrasts and similarities between the Jewish and Mennonite communities are quite interesting. With regard to intermarriage the Jewish and Mennonite communities have traditionally taken a negative position. Recently more Jews and Mennonites are marrying outside the faith. While the Jewish community is very concerned with the high rate of intermarriage, the Mennonite community seems little concerned. Shouldn't this concern Mennonites for whom the primary means of church growth has been what is commonly known as "bedroom evangelism"?

3. One way Muppie couples have dealt with their partriarchal patterns is by hiring someone to do the cleaning and household chores for them; thus they appear to be liberated.

4. Deciding if, when, and how many children to have is a very conflicting experience for Muppies. They very much want to continue their aspiring ways, but also want to be in the family way. It is difficult to advance the careers of two adults, plus enhance the lives of one or two children.

   While in the past husbands could pursue their careers while their wives raised the children (as was the case in many First Wave Muppie families), that is not the case today. Today both Muppie spouses have increased aspirations and expectations: Muppie husbands hope to be both professionals and fathers, and Muppie wives hope to be both mothers and professionals. Some have suggested, however, that a dual career couple with children and a farm couple with children have significant similarities. But somehow programming the computer as a family is different than planting corn as a family.

Therapy
Interview

CONFIDENTIAL:

Transcript of Psychotherapy Screening Interview, Dr. Jacob Hoffman with Pastor Samuel Groff

Dr: Hello, what brings you here today?

SG: I haven't been able to eat lately and I've had a lot of headaches.

Dr: How long has this been happening?

SG: Mainly in the last 6 months, but off and on for 2 years.

Dr: Why did you decide to come and see me now?

SG: Well I went to Dr. Yoder, my family doctor, but he said there was nothing he could do, and he believed it was nerves. Also my wife has been after me for a long time to see a psychologist. She thinks a lot of things are bothering me and that I won't open up enough. Also my bishop thought it would be a good idea for me to come . . .

Dr: Your bishop?

SG: Yes, you see . . . I am the pastor at the North Oak Avenue Mennonite Church.

Dr: Oh, really, a Mennonite church! How long have you been a pastor?

SG: I have been at North Oak for four years, but before then I was a pastor for 30 years in Harrisonburg.

Dr: How is it going, being the pastor at North Oak?

SG: The first year was great, but the last 3 years have not gone so well . . .

Dr: What has been the problem?

SG: North Oak is an older Mennonite congregation and a lot of people commute into the church from the surrounding areas. Well, in the last couple of years there have been a lot of young Mennonites moving into the North Oak area to live and they have been coming to our church.

Dr: What's the problem? I would think you would like more people to come to your church.

SG: Yes, that is what I thought as well, so I tried to make them feel as welcome as possible and did a lot of things to have them come to the congregation.

Dr: So I still don't understand the problem?

SG: One of the first problems was that these new people wanted all the benches taken out of the church and folding chairs put in in their place. They had all kinds of theological, psychological, and social reasons why the benches should be removed. To hear them talk, having benches is a rejection of everything Christian and Mennonite.

They keep quoting all their people with long German-sounding names. I have been trying to read some of these theologians, but honestly, I don't understand a word of it.

I feel like I am going crazy. These people talk about how great these theologians are and I don't understand any of it. I'm starting to think that I'm not very bright . . . But I did have almost two years of seminary. I'm starting to doubt my own abilities.

Dr: What do the people who have been in the congregation for a long time think?

SG: They are even more confused and frustrated than I am! They think that a lot of these people are confused and irrational. They've been putting more and more pressure on me to straighten out these new people. They think it's crazy to remove the benches. The congregation just got new benches 10 years ago and we just finished paying them off. The older members think it is a wiser use of money to keep the benches, plus they like the benches and see no reason for removing them.

The new people, however, continue to talk about how the benches symbolize a linear, patriarchal, Catholic, hierarchical, militaristic approach to church life, and that the church should not represent these things and that it is not a good witness. They feel embarrassed

to bring their friends to church.

I really feel in the middle of this. I think this is when I started to get headaches . . . But I don't know how you can help me. To me this seems like a church problem.

Dr: Sometimes it helps to talk with someone else about your problems.

SG: You know, Dr., that is the same thing a lot of the new people say. In fact, they think everybody should be in a small group. They keep talking about community, accountability, support, and sharing. However, when I have attended their groups the discussion is usually about political issues or theological double-talk.

Dr: That's very interesting.

SG: Then about 6 months ago we had a big blow-up between the two groups at church and that is when I stopped eating and my headaches got worse!

Dr: What was the blow-up about?

SG: Well, the older people in the congregation wanted to have a 3-part tele-communication seminar with a well-known preacher from North Carolina.

Dr: I don't understand.

SG: Well, this preacher has one of those new satellites which can beam a live program from one place to another. The long-time members wanted to have a big screen up front and have this preacher speak, instead of having the sermon for four weeks. The preacher was doing a series on the biblical principles of a successful Christian life.

Dr: What did you think about all of this?

SG: Well, I felt a little threatened by it, but on the whole I thought it was a good idea. I think a congregation needs new ideas and variety.

But these new people were totally against it. I was really shocked. They said high technology did not belong in the church. They said we were a *gemeinschaft,* not a *gesellschaft.* You would have thought they were Amish and against technology the way they talked.

The thing that really confuses me is that these people use technology at home. It seems so odd. For example, when I call most of them I get a phone-answering machine. When I visit them at home they usually have to turn off their VCR and make me a cup of coffee with their digital radio/TV clock coffee-maker. When I visit the long-time members, many have little technology in their homes, except out in the barns.

It has gotten pretty bad at church. The new people are threatening to leave. They say that unless we start processing and resolving these issues they will not stay. They keep talking about needing a congregational model which facilitates positive problem-solving and strategizing. I don't know what they are talking about. But I am afraid we are in the middle of a split. . . .

Dr: Can't you understand why these new people would be so upset?

SG: Well, no, not really! I think it is best to use simple speech. I don't know if you are a Christian, Dr., but Jesus said that your yea should be yea . . . .

Dr: Yes, but sometimes things are very complex and can't be stated simply . . . .

SG: Well, I think we should learn to communicate better. If we can't talk in simple terms and learn to understand each other we are in deep trouble. Don't you agree, Dr., that communication is important?

Dr: Unquestionably! Verbal and nonverbal interpersonal communication and exchange is imperative and mandatory for functional and self-actualizing behavior . . . .

SG: I'm sorry, I think I missed you. What was that again?

Dr: Well, I guess I got carried away. Pastor Groff, I have something I think we should talk about before we continue . . . .

SG: What is it, Dr. Hoffman? Do you think there is anything you can do for me?

Dr: Well, I am not sure . . . you . . . I am a Mennonite . . . .

SG: Is that right? I didn't realize that. Well good, then maybe you can better understand what I am going through.

Dr: Well, I am not sure. You see . . . I attend the Community Mennonite Fellowship of Oakland.

SG: You mean that new community church in center city that recently split from First Mennonite?

Dr: Yes, that's right.

SG: A lot of the new people at North Oak have said they like your fellowship and some have left to go there. So I guess you know a lot of them?

Dr: Yes, that's right. So I think it might be a conflict of interest, and I think it would be best for me to refer you to someone else.

SG: Well, if you think so, Dr.

Dr: I would like to recommend Dr. Ira Kauffman.

SG: Is he from the Kauffman family in Ohio?

Dr: No, pastor, he's from the Kauffman family in Brooklyn.

SG: Oh, I don't know any Kauffmans in Brooklyn.

Dr: Oh, I'm sorry, you misunderstand. Dr. Kauffman is Jewish, not Mennonite. He's likely to be able to help you more than I can.

Glossary of Commonly Used Muppie Words

Affirm: To compliment ("I would like to affirm you in your role as coordinator.").

Center (centered): To be emotionally and spiritually healthy ("She is a very centered person.").

Energy: Commitment ("Do you have any energy for this project?").

Global Awareness: To have travelled to another country, like international food and have a lot of international art objects. ("Paul and Linda seem to have a lot of global awareness.").

Focused: Narrow-minded ("He seems like a very focused person.").

Identify: To feel sorry for someone ("I can sure identify with you.").

Networking: To be friendly and sociable to others. ("John was doing a lot of networking at the party.").

Prioritize: To put first things first. ("The Worship Committee prioritized their agenda.").

State-of-the-art: Most advanced technology. ("The new tractor is state-of-the-art.").

For Non-Mennonites

Anabaptists: The left wing of the Reformation, also known as the Swiss Brethren and Radical Reformers. The name was given by their opponents because adult baptism, and not infant baptism, was a distinguishing characteristic. Mennonites trace their historical and theological roots to the Anabaptists.

Conrad Grebel: An early and influential Anabaptist leader.

Mennonite Church: The largest and oldest Mennonite body in North America. Also known as the "Old Mennonites."

Mennonite Central Committee (MCC): International relief, development, and service organization supported by many Mennonite groups.

Mennonite Quarterly Review: A scholarly journal which focuses on Anabaptist and Mennonite theology, history and life.

Voluntary Service: A period of time, usually from three months to two years, given to working without pay, often in health services, education, or development.

Sojourners: A radical non-Mennonite monthly publication which focuses on justice, peace, community, and theology.

Shoo-fly pie: A favorite Mennonite pastry and dessert (molasses, soda, flour, shortening, and brown sugar).

About the Author—Emerson L. Lesher is a 32-year-old who, for the past 15 years, has lived, studied, or worked in the following cities—Grantham, PA; Harrisburg, PA; Los Angeles, CA; and Philadelphia, PA. He currently lives in the city of Lancaster, PA. His credits include showing the Grand Champion Steer at the New York State Fair, getting married in 1975, writing numerous articles and papers in geropsychology and being a psychologist at the Philadelphia Geriatric Center. Dr. Lesher is currently a gerontologist at Philhaven Hospital. He is a member of the East Chestnut Street Mennonite Church where he is facilitator of small groups. Dr. Lesher received a score of 110 on the Muppie Scale.